Translators
Alex Mizuno
Akira Watanabe

Editors
Dominic Mah
Nicole Curry

Production Artists
Yoann Resmond
Yuki Chung

US Cover Design
Yuki Chung

Lettering Fonts
Comicraft
www.comicbookfonts.com

President
Robin Kuo

First volume published
January 15, 1999 in Japan by
Shonen Gahosha Co., Ltd
ISBN4-7859-1883-7

Publisher
ComicsOne Corporation
47257 Fremont Blvd.
Fremont, CA 94538
www.ComicsOne.com

First Edition: March 2001
ISBN 1-58899-072-9

SARAI 2

TABLE OF CONTENTS

SARAI 2

WORK 2
The Village of Stone 5

ERR...
Uhö
WHA-
WHAT'S WRONG, MR. AULOX?
RUN, BELASCO!!

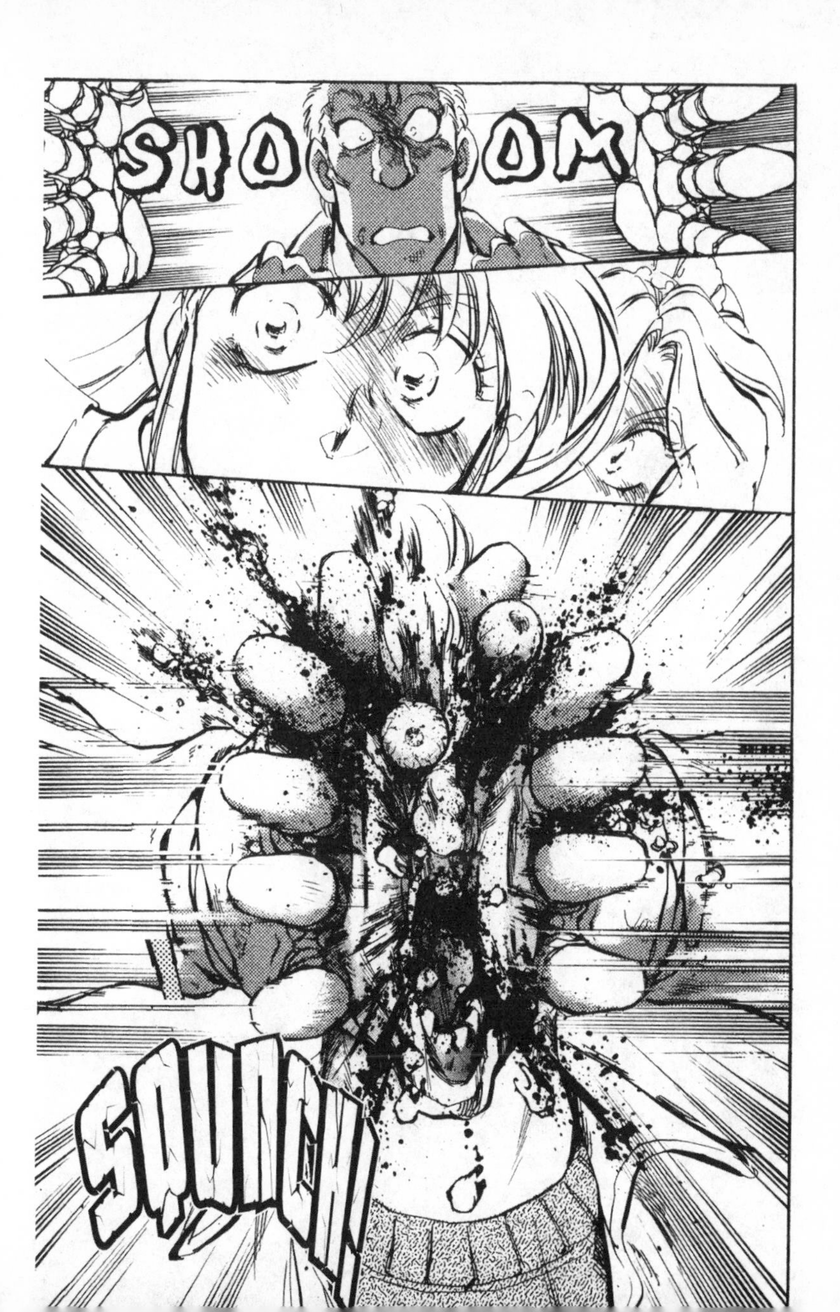
SHO OM
SQUNCH!

THUD
SPLASH
SPLUGH
WAH

THE STONE ZOMBIE!
THAT'S THE-
IT'S
EEEEEEE!
ZHHM
GASP

SARAI!
FLICKER!!
NO...
HEE
ARG!
NO!
NO!
NOOO!
STOP!

KSHANG!
RICH-
ELLE!
THE
BELT!!
CLANG!
CUT THE BELT,
RICHELLE!!
TIIIN
QWAKIIIN
KLAAANG
GWOHHH
CARAMAS!
GIVE
ME
THAT!

NOW'S OUR CHANCE!
LET'S GO, CARAMAS!
YES SIR
GNOHHH
GET BEHIND IT AND CUT THE MAIDS' BELTS!
I'LL DO IT!!
BAROSSO!
IT'S THE ONLY PLACE YOU CAN STAB!!
AIM BETWEEN THE STONES!!
!!
HAHA HAHA
HA...
SKWEEZ
SKWEEZ
WHAT'S THIS, MR. AULOX?
WHA...

RICHELLE! BAROSSO!
A SECOND ONE !
WAAAAAAH

ZH.
BWAP
ZZZHOOOM
CRUNCH
TCH.
WATCH
YOURSELF.

IT CAN'T REACH ITS BACK, AND...
IT'S SLOW ...
DON'T FRET !!
RICHELLE!!
TOK
HE'S SEEN YOU!
GROK
CAREFUL !
ALMOST ...
AH...

GAAAAAWWWW!

THUD
DAMN YOU, BAROSSO!!
FWAM!
CHOOM
OH, HE'S MAD...!!

GWAK
IT'S-
IT'LL CRUSH ALL OF US!!

FLMP
CRACK
SPLAT
CRACK

WHAT...
WHAT'S GOING ON?
CRACK
SPLAT
CRACH
BLIP
CRACK

WHAT THE...?!
END OF WORK: 2 - 5

WORK 2
The Village of Stone 6

SARAI
SGooo
Huff
Huff
Huff
Huff

KKKKKKK
SCREECH

SPLASH
WE FAILED.
SSSHHH
WE DIDN'T PROTECT YOU.
I TOLD YOU NOT TO WORRY.
IT WAS MY FAULT FOR TELLING YOU NOT TO RESIST.
WE PUT YOU IN DANGER ...
AND YOU HAD TO SAVE US...
......
YOU PROTECTED ME IN THE END.
BUT ...

SARAI!
FLICKER!
YES, MA' AM.
!!
HANDS ON THE WALL!
STICK 'EM OUT!

HIGHER!
LIFT YOUR BUT-TOCKS!
EEP

SLAP!
SMAK!
SLAP
KYAH!
OWW!
NOW, WASH UP!
DON'T LEAVE ANY MESS.
WE'RE SQUARE NOW, RIGHT?
YES MA' AM
Y...
ALL RIGHT?
NOW YOU'RE FORGIV-EN!
SO NO MORE MOANING!
THROB

WOW, COOL.
I FEEL SO ♡ STOIC NOW.
THEY MIGHT BE A LITTLE MUSTY.

WHAT OF IT, GUARD MAID?

IS THIS TRUE?
AS SHE SAYS?
BAROSSO!
YOU NEVER TOLD ME THAT!
SHE JUST MADE IT UP!
DON'T LISTEN TO HER!

YOU'VE LIVED 10 YEARS MORE THAN MOST PEOPLE.
YOU'VE ENJOYED ALL THE BENEFITS.
STOMP
HOW...
... CAN YOU CALL THIS "LIVING!"

YOU SAID IF I TOOK THE PILLS,
I COULD LIVE ON FOR A WHILE.
DID YOU MEAN ...

LIVING THE REST OF MY DAYS WITH A BODY OF STONE?!

THOSE WHO KEEP TAKING THE PILLS
TURN INTO THOSE PEGMATITES, DON'T THEY?!
AM I RIGHT?
THEY SAY YOUR DRUG "NOBLE ORIGIN"
...DOES NOT WORK FOR EVERY-ONE.
DEPEN-DING ON THE INDI-VIDUAL ...
IT CAN BRING HORROR INSTEAD OF HOPE.
AND THE GMA-TITES ...
AREN'T LIKE THE GIGANTS. IT'S NOT NORMAL TO GROW SO HUGE IN A SINGLE BODY.
T'S HE IDE FECT
OF NOBLE ORIGIN.
BARO-SSO, YOU'RE FROM
"OLSO," AREN'T YOU?

THE PEGA-TITES
HAVE NO HUMAN CONSCIO-USNESS ...
AS THEIR AWARENESS FADES...
ONLY THEIR HATE FOR LIVING HUMANS REMAINS.
THEY FEEL REGRET FOR TAKING THE PILLS...
...BUT THEY DO HAVE A STRONG ANIMOSITY TOWARD HUMANS.
...AND HATRED FOR THE HUMANS WHO SELL THE PILLS.

I DON'T KNOW WHAT MY PREDE-CESSORS HAVE DONE.
BUT FOR WHAT I'VE DONE, I DESERVE GRATITUDE, NOT RESENT-MENT.
GUYS LIKE YOU ...
ARE ALL THE SAME!
"OLSO" IS A PHAR-MACEU-TICAL SYNDI-CATE.
YOU GUYS PROFIT FROM PEOPLE'S FEAR.
YOU SELL DANGEROUS PILLS SO YOU CAN DOMINATE THEIR HOPES..
AND THEIR MINDS !!
HEH!
WHAT ABUSE!
WE'RE TRYING TO WIN BACK MANKIND'S FUTURE.
WE DON'T TAKE LIP FROM MAIDS LIKE YOU.

BATTLE MAIDS ...
WHO DO YOU TRUST,
MR. AULOX ?
... ARE NOT HUMAN !
THEY PRETEND TO BE INNOCENT GIRLS, BUT-
HIDDEN PHYSICAL SKILLS!
SUPER STRENGTH !
IN TRUTH THEY ARE...
VICIOUS KILLING MACHINES !!

I ADMIT THAT.
SURE, N.O. ISN'T PERFECT YET.
AS PART OF OUR CONTINUOUS EFFORT TO MAKE IMPROVEMENTS.
BUT THAT'S EXACTLY WHY WE'VE COLLECTED CLINICAL DATA
WHO SPEAKS FOR YOU?
WATCHDOGS HIRED FOR MONEY TO OBEY THEIR MASTERS?
OR A MAN OF MEDICINE WHO GIVES HOPE TO A PLAGUED PEOPLE?
FEH. COLLECTING DATA?!
WITH CUSTOMERS AS GUINEA PIGS?!
N.O. IS A DRUG WITH A FUTURE!
IT COULD FREE ALL HUMANS FROM A GROTESQUE FATE!!
BAM!

WE MUST ACCEPT CERTAIN RISKS!
THAT'S THE PRICE YOU HAVE TO PAY!!
YOU TALK TOUGH, AS USUAL ...
BAROSSO, MICHELLE.
NICE TO SEE YOU AGAIN.

IT'S SO GOOD TO SEE YOU,
MOTHER!
BUMP
MOTHER WISTABLE!
HELP ME, MOTHER!!
YOU CAN HELP ME,
CAN'T YOU?!
YOU CAN DO SOMETHING!
WITH THAT POWER OF YOURS
MR. AULOX ...

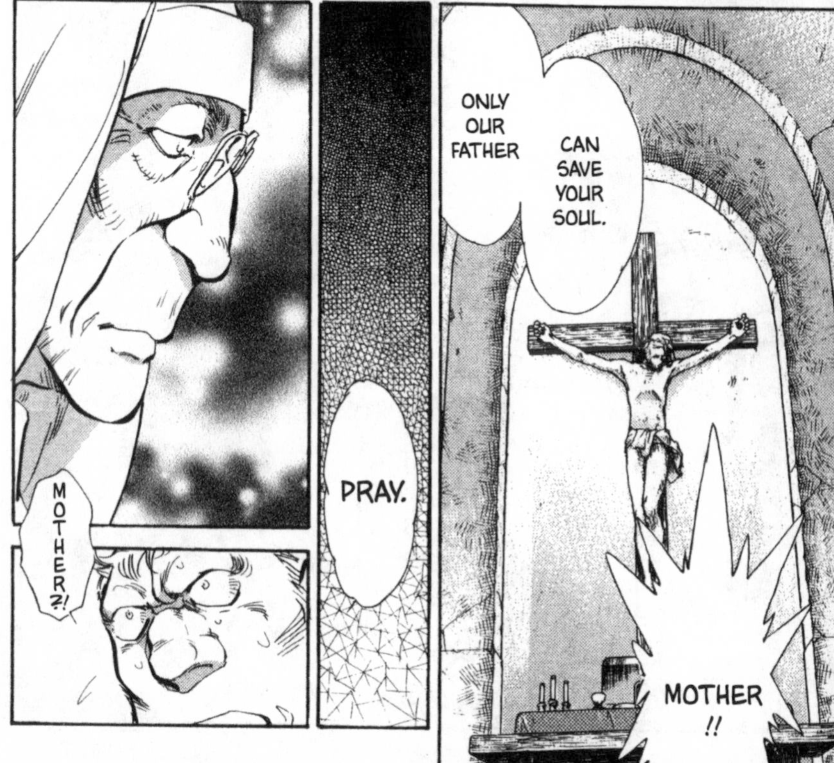
ONLY OUR FATHER
CAN SAVE YOUR SOUL.
MOTHER !!
PRAY.
MOTHER?!

END OF WORK: 2 - 6

WORK 2
The Village of Stone 7

UH
CRUMBLE
EYE-BATS EAT UP CORPSES INSTANTLY.
SO CLEAN !
YOU
THINK SO?

CRKL
CRKL
IT'S NOT THAT GROSS.
JUST LEAVE THE PEGMATITES.
WELL, AT LEAST WITH NO FLESH LEFT
THEY'RE JUST
NAMELESS STONES NOW.

SURE.
...WITH THIS UNPLEA-SANT WORK.
THANK YOU FOR YOUR HELP.
THESE MUST'VE BEEN HIS FAITHFUL MEN.
SO SELFISH ...
THAT'S HOW HE IS!!
OOPS
LOUSE !!
SHAMELESS
I WONDER WHY MR. AULOX ISN'T HERE.

BAM
BAM
PASSING BEHIND.
OK.

WSH
WSH
WSH

N...
NO!
C'MON,
FLONTE, I CAN'T WAIT ANY MORE!
NO.
WE CAN'T. NOT HERE.
Huff
Huff
LET'S WAIT, TUPE.
OK?
WE CAN DO IT THE RIGHT WAY.
I HAVE TO GET BACK BEFORE WE'RE CAUGHT.
TOO LATE!
EEEK
CHIEF!
GET BACK TO WORK RIGHT NOW!
HYAAAAAA!

GRMBL
NOO!
YEEK!
WHERE DO YOU THINK YOU ARE!
HONESTLY!
PEGENTO FLA (12 YEARS OLD)
GYU?!
WHAT DO YOU WANT?
THIS ISN'T A PLACE FOR YOU GUYS!!

MY NEW CARD.
AS OF TODAY, I'M THE BOSS HERE.
SEE?
THAT'S BULL!!
GRIN GRIN
ONLY GROWN-UPS CAN BE BOSSES.
YOU'RE SUPPOSED TO BE WORKING AT THE MINE.
HEE HEE
I'M TAKING MIGUEL'S PLACE.
THE DIRTY WORK AT THE MINE IS NOT FOR AN ELITE LIKE ME.
RING
NO WAY! YOU'RE THE SAME AGE AS ME!!
DON'T TALK LIKE YOU'RE SOME BIG SHOT!!
FROM NOW ON, YOU'RE ALL UNDER MY SUPER-VISION.
SLACK OFF AND IT'S 100 LASHES.
GYU AULOX (12 YEARS OLD)
WHAT?!

I'LL CHECK YOUR GROUP FIRST.
I WON'T ACCEPT IT!
EVER!
IT'S NOT RIGHT!
GYU!!
EH, PEG-ENTO?
ALWAYS THE SASSY MOUTH ...
SLOPPY JOB!
THIS IS STILL DIRTY!
SKWEEZ

THAT'S A LIE!!
YOU JUST TOUCHED IT WITH YOUR DIRTY PAWS!!
WASH THEM ALL AGAIN!
THE CHIEF GETS 30 LASHES FOR DISPUTING ME!
I'VE WANTED THIS FOR A LONG TIME.
FWIP
OH YES.
ARE YOU SERIOUS?
WAIT!
GYU!
EEK!
HOLD HER AND EXPOSE HER BUTT!

CLOP
CLOP
AMONG THE SHORT-LIVED RESIDENTS OF FIOLITO THERE ARE MARRIED COUPLES, BUT NO CONCEPT OF FAMILIES.
FEW PARENTS LIVE TO SEE THEIR CHIDREN GROW UP.
THE MONASTERY USED TO BE THE FARM...
BAROSSO AND I GREW UP THERE.
IT'S A FARM.
ALL THE VILLAGE CHILDREN ARE SENT HERE.
THIS IS A FACTORY WHERE THE ELDER GROUP TAKES VARIOUS JOBS TO MAKE A LIVING.
HM ...
SO MANY KIDS.

EXTREMELY INDEPEND-ENT CHILDREN MATURE EARLY.
OFTEN, THEY BEAR A CHILD AT THE AGE OF 12 OR 13.
SLAP
HAHAHA. LOOK AT YOU, PEGENTO.
DO YOU WANT TO KNEEL ANL APOLOGIZE FOR TALKIN BACK TO ME?
WHIP

HEH.
YOU'RE A TOUGH GIRL.
SLAP SLAP
NEVER!
SKWEEZ
EEK
I'LL NEVER DO THAT!
SPLASH
SOONER OR LATER ...
YOU'LL CRY FOR MERCY.

MANUELLA!!
TO BE CHILD-LESS AT 18.
IN THIS VILLAGE, IT'S A CRIME...
MICHELLE!!

DEAR ...
WHERE'S MOTHER?
DIDN'T YOU BRING HER WITH YOU?
...
WHY?
YOU COULDN'T DRAG HER OUT?
GUARD MAIDS?!

IF YOU DO
DON'T SHOW YOURSELF AROUND MOTHER AGAIN.
YOU TAKE YOUR CHANCES WITH US.

RMBL
RMBL

KRANGG
GRIP
I HAVE A FATHER AND A MOTHER!
I'M NOT LIKE YOU STRAY CATS AND DOGS!
YOU DON'T EVEN KNOW YOUR PARENTS!!
AND YOUR LIVES ARE SHORT, JUST LIKE CATS AND DOGS.
SMACK SMACK
SMACK
HOW DARE YOU DEFY ME!!
STOP, GYU!!
YOU'RE GONNA KILL HIM!!
IT'S ALL HIS FAULT!
THIS STUPID KID!!
BOP BUMP
BONK THUD
HE'S TAKING THOSE WEIRD PILLS!

MR. GYU!
MR. GYU!
HE WANTS YOU BACK RIGHT AWAY!
MY FATHER?
YES, HE SAID IT'S URGENT.
HMPH!
YOU GET OFF EASY TODAY, MANUELLA.
I'LL FINISH WITH YOU LATER.
PEGENTO.

DAD!
I'M HOME.
I'M HOME, DAD.
WHERE ARE YOU?
DAD?
MOM?
THE BEROOM ?
YOO HOO ...?

?!!
END OF WORK 2 - 7

WORK 2
The Village of Stone 8

DAD!
MOM!

MOM!!
AAG ...
KKKK
DAD!!
UHH
DAD!!
WAAAAHHH!

FWAP
W-
WAIT!
THAP
HOLD IT!!
YEEEEK!
MR. AULOX !
MRS. AULOX !!

?
OH
NO
HORSE
MARKET?
WHAT
IS IT?
EH?

WHAT D' YOU THINK YOU'RE DOING ?
I'LL REPORT YOU DITCHING WORK!
HEAVY CARRIAGE HORSES ARE SO COOL.
YOU GO AHEAD, SARAI!
FLICKER !!
DON'T BE A PRUDE.
SO BIG AND POWER-FUL.
I JUST WANNA LOOK. ♡
I'LL BE BACK SOON.
WE SCARED THE VILLAGE HEAD. WE HAVE NOTHING TO WORRY ABOUT!
PEGMATITES ONLY COME OUT AT NIGHT, RIGHT?
AH, DAMN.
WAIT
FLICKER!
EVEN IF WE RETURN NOW, THERE'S JUST THE MAID WORK TO DO.

I SHOULD FIND OUT HOW FAR OLSO HAS EXPANDED.
MAYBE I SHOULD GO CHECK OUT THE WEST VALLEY.
BOY, SHE'S REALLY BUBBLY.

WHAT?! THEY WERE KILLED WITH A SWORD ?!
WHA
GYU'S FATHER AND MOTHER ?!

THEY SAID THE ROOM WAS LIKE A POOL OF BLOOD!!
THEY SAY THE KILLER WAS A GUARD MAID THE NUNS HIRED!
I HEARD HIS MOM'S BELLY WAS CUT OPEN!
WHAT?
SHE WAS PREGNANT!!
WHA
WHAT'S A GUARD MAID?
THEY SERVE THEIR CLIENTS AS MAIDS AND BODY-GUARDS.
THEY'RE WOMEN, BUT THEY ARE ALSO UNNATU-RALLY SKILLED FIGHTING MACHINES.
WHERE DID YOU HEAR ALL THAT?
THEY KILLED THE AULOXS?
ALL THE GROWN-UPS
ARE TALK-ING ABOUT IT.
IT'S BIG NEWS IN THE VILLAGE.

SIGH
GORGEOUS ♡

HOW MUCH IS THIS SHIRE?

ARE YOU SERIOUS, MISS?
THAT ONE?

YOU GOTTA THINK THIS OVER.
YOU'RE TOO SHORT TO RIDE THIS HORSE.
YOU WANNA USE A LADDER TO CLIMB UP EACH TIME?

NOW, HOW ABOUT THIS CUTE PONY?
PERFECT SIZE FOR YOU.
MFF

Thump

STOMP

BRRRR

EASY, EASY.
DID I SCARE YOU?
I'M SORRY.

THAT'S AMAZING!
SHUT UP!
OH.
MY. GOD!

NOW YOU KNOW.
HAHA

LIKE A CIRCUS MONKEY SITTING ON A HORSE.

USUALLY, THE DEALER'S FIRST OFFER IS NOT REALLY FAIR, I KNOW.
AHEM! AND ABOUT THE PRICE...

!?
IS THIS A JOKE?
WHAT NOW?
WHERE DID YOU HIDE THE BABY?
WHERE IS IT?
YOU KILLER MAID!!
SHUT UP!
WHA...
AND RIPPED HIS BABY FROM HIS WIFE'S BELLY!
YOU KILLED MR. AULOX
DON'T PLAY DUMB!!

KRAANG
KLAANG
GASP
STOP IT!!
CRACK!
CRACK
WHAT THE HELL ARE YOU TALKING ABOUT!
WOW.
DAMN IT!
BEAT HER DOWN!

BONK
AUGH!
THUD
WHAM
WHO IS THIS GIRL?
W H A
YOU KNOW NOTHING, HUH?
EXPLAIN YOURSELF!
DON'T MAKE A BATTLE MAID MAD.
YOU SAW ME,
DIDN'T YOU?!

F...
FRANTZ?

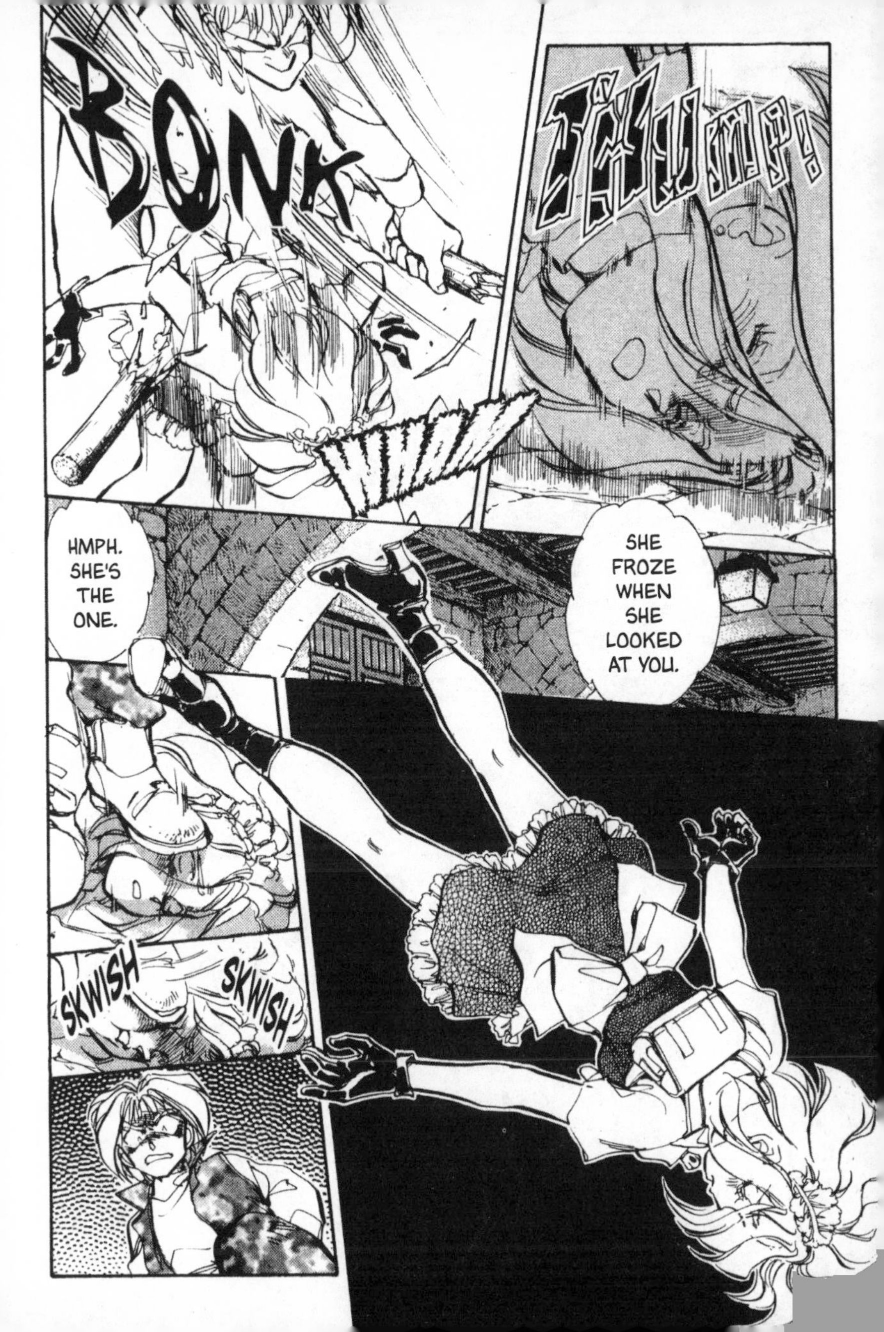
BONK
SHE FROZE WHEN SHE LOOKED AT YOU.
HMPH. SHE'S THE ONE.
SKWISH
SKWISH

CHILDREN
WORK IN
THE FARM,
TOO.

AS LONG AS THEIR LIFE HAS MEANING...

...AND THEY THINK OF IT AS A NORMAL LIFETIME...

...THEY DON'T NEED TO USE N.O.

BUT AS LONG AS THERE'S HATE AND GREED IN THE OLD WORLD...

THOSE OBSESSED WITH LIVING, THOSE ATTACHED TO THIS WORLD, MUST NOT CROSS THIS BRIDGE.
THOSE WHO SET OUT FOR THE VALLEY MUST PURIFY THEIR MIND, AND ABANDON ALL BONDS TO THE LAND OF LIVING.
END OF WORK 2 - 8

WORK 2
The Village of Stone 9

ALL WHO SET OUT FOR THE VALLEY OF SANCTUARY MUST PURIFY THEIR MIND AND ABANDON ALL BONDS TO THE LAND OF LIVING. THOSE OBSESSED WITH LIVING IN THE MATERIAL WORLD MUST NOT CROSS THIS BRIDGE.
....
SEEMS LIKE THE HORSE MUST'VE RETURNED HERE.
I SHOULD GET AWAY FROM THIS PLACE ...

WHA ...
WHAT ARE THESE?
COULD IT BE ...?
GASP
PEGMATITES!!
THEY'RE ALIVE!!

BRRRR

MOTHER ... THE MONA-STERY ...
THEY'RE TAKING IN PEG-MATITES!
AH
SQUEEZE
DAMN!
WHY?
WHY HIDE THE TRUTH?!
WHY?
WHY DIDN'T THEY TELL ME?!

IS THAT TRUE?
WHY WOULD I LIE?
KAPP
KAPP
I COULDN'T TELL YOU 'CAUSE YOU WERE AT MICHELLE'S PUB.
I MET THEM.
THEY CAME INTO THE VILLAGE ...

OH, DEAR.
GOODESS!

YOU N'T DO THAT LONE.
WE'LL HELP YOU.
SO THEY LIFTED THE CARRIAGE.
AND THEY DID IT QUICKLY.
THEY EEMED TRANGE AT FIRST.
BUT THEY WERE VERY KIND.
YOU OK?
THEY SAID THEY WERE GOING TO THE MONASTERY.
SO I SHOWED THEM THE WAY.
DIDN'T THINK THEY'D DO A THING LIKE
PULL A BABY OUT OF A MOTH-ER'S BELLY.
....
....

SO HE CAN TREAT US LIKE ANIMALS.
GYU JUST USES THEIR INFLU-ENCE
IT'S TRUE, WE DON'T KNOW OUR PARENTS
YOU KNOW
THAT JUST MAKES HIM THE SAME AS US.
KLUPP
KUPP
NOW HE'S LOST HIS MOM AND DAD.
BUT WHAT'S SO GREAT ABOUT
HAV-ING TWO PARE-NTS?
I DON'T HAVE
ANY SYMPATHY FOR GYU!
I CAN'T SIT DOWN RIGHT 'CAUSE MY BUTT HURTS!
I CAN'T HELP IT!
HONE-STLY!
YOU'VE BEEN RUBBING IT UP ON ME.
YOU WANTED TO RIDE UP FRONT.
FLUSH
UM
ARE YOU
POKING AT MY BUTT?

RMBL
RMBL
RMBL
IT WAS SIX YEARS AGO.
THE NIGHT OF THE HARVEST FESTIVAL.

IN THE VILLAGE OF STONE, FIELD CROPPING IS EXTREMELY HARD.
SO THE JOY OF THE HAR-VEST IS OVER-WHELMING.
THIS GARDEN IS RUINED NOW, AS YOU CAN SEE.
BUT ON THAT NIGHT, ADULTS AND CHILDREN DANCED IN A CIRCLE HERE. THEIR FACES WERE LIT BY THE FIRE AND EVERYBODY SEEMED HAPPY.
AND WE WERE REALLY LOOKING FORWARD TO IT.
FOR DAYS WE'D PREPARED FOR THE FESTIVAL

NOBODY BELIEVED THAT THOSE WHO SET OUT FOR THE VALLEY OF SANCTUARY
RMBL
RMBL
WOULD EVER RETURN.
BUT
IF HE'S BEEN INVOLVED WITH OLSO SINCE THAT TIME -
HE MUST'VE BEEN THE ONLY MAN IN THE VIL-LAGE WHO KNEW THE TRUTH.
GREAT !!
NOW WHAT AM I GONNA DO?!
END OF WORK 2 - 9
WHO'D HAVE PRE-DICTED ...
IT WOULD TURN INTO A NIGHT OF HORROR.
WHKRAK
GRKL
GRKL
GRKL
GRKL

BUT WHEN THEY SAW THE HARVEST FESTIVAL, WHICH JOYFULLY PRAISES LIFE... THEY FELT THEIR LAST REMAINING LINK TO HUMANITY WAS BEING SEVERED.
THEY WERE VERY AFRAID OF BEING SEEN.
NORMALLY THEY WOULDN'T APPEAR IN FRONT OF A CROWD.
STILL THEY RECOGNIZED MOTHER'S VOICE.
THEY WENT BACK...
AND THE VILLAGE PEOPLE THOUGHT
THAT MOTHER WAS CONTROLLING THE CREATURES.
GUS AULOX CALLED MOTHER A WITCH!!
FOR THE VILAGERS,
THE BEAST HAD EXISTED ONLY IN GOSSIP.
THAT NIGHT IT BECAME A HORRIFIC REALITY.

WORK 2
The Village of Stone 10

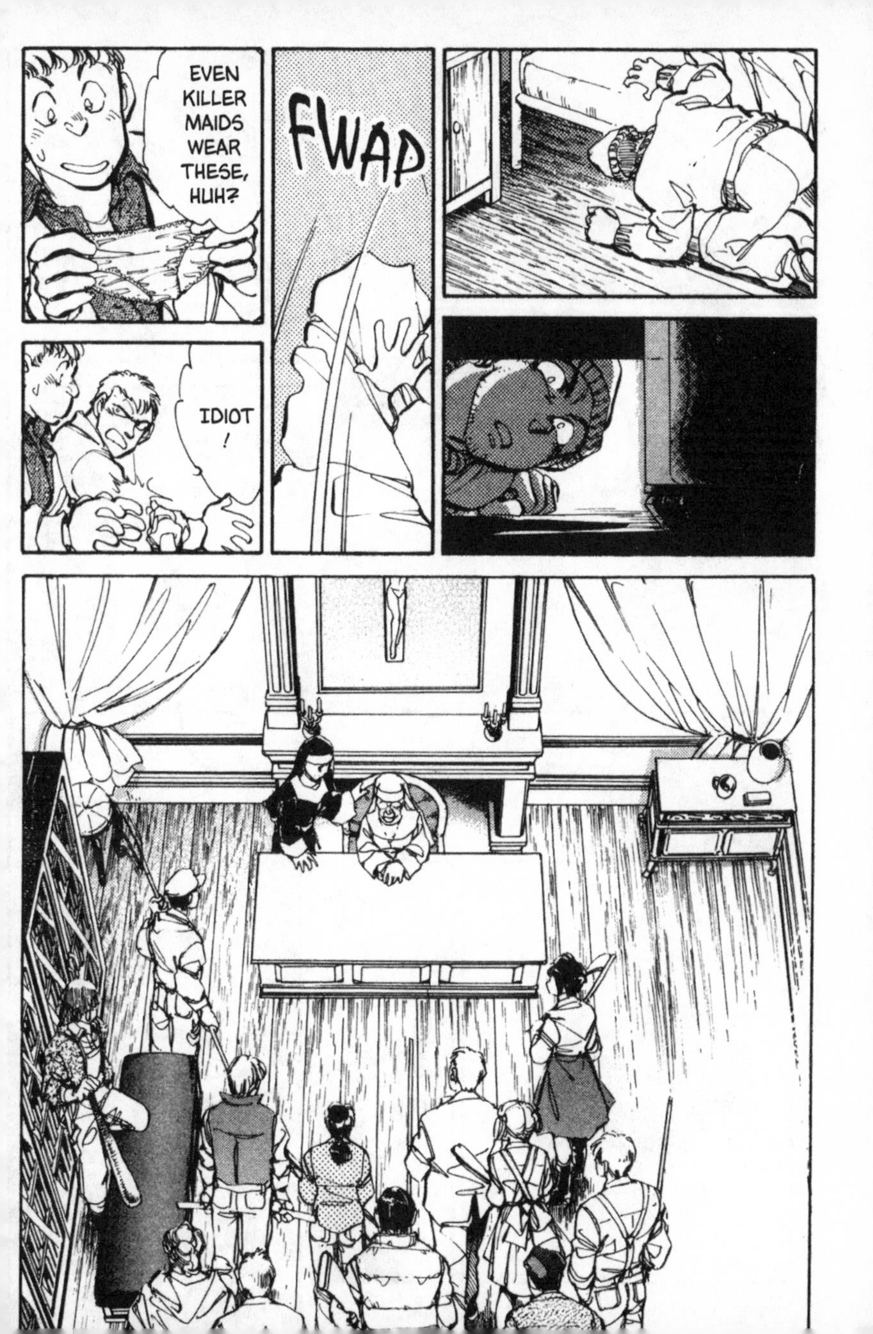
EVEN KILLER MAIDS WEAR THESE, HUH?
IDIOT !
FWAP

THE ONE I SAW WAS
THE OTHER ONE.
WE'LL GET HER.
WE'LL HANG 'EM TOGETHER.
THEY SAY YOU LIKE HORSES.
EH, FLICKER?
SORRY IT'S NOT A HOBBY HORSE.
SLAP
NNNFF

IMPOSSIBLE!!
THEY WOULD NOT
DO SUCH A THING!
IMPOSSIBLE?!
WAP
IMPOSSIBLE?!
WAP
IMPOSSIBL?!
WAP
WHUMP!
OOF

YOU SAY IT'S IMPOSSIBLE?!
WAP
MY PARENTS WERE KILLED RIGHT BEFORE MY EYES!
IT COULDN'T HAPPEN?
WAP
GYU!!
DON'T HIT A HELPLESS WOMAN!
S-
STOP IT!!
WHY WOULD WE KILL MR. AULOX?!
WHY ...
YOU TOLD THEM TO DO IT, DIDN'T YOU!
YOU HIRED THOSE MAIDS!!
SHUT UP!!
CALM DOWN!!
CALM DOWN, GYU!!

YOU CAN'T THINK STRAIGHT WHEN YOU'RE MAD.
SHUT UP!! SHUT UP!!
DON'T TELL ME WHAT TO DO!
YOU OLD WITCH!!
I'LL NEVER LISTEN TO YOU!!
YOU CAN'T FOOL ME!!
EVERYONE KNOWS YOU HATED MR. AULOX.
HE CALLED YOU A WITCH
AND CLOSED YOUR MONASTERY.
HE WAS RESPONSIBLE FOR YOUR EXILE. HOW COULD YOU NOT HATE HIM?.
MM
MMF
MFFF!

HURRY BACK, SARAI.
YOU'LL BE SORRY FOR OPENING YOUR SMART MOUTH TO ME.

WE FOUND IT, BAROSSO!
IT WAS UNDER THEIR BED!
WHAT?!
MMF

YOUR BROTHER.
LOOK, GYU...
....
MOTHER!

I...
...HAVE A BAD FEEL-ING ABOUT THIS.
THE KIND OF FEELING ...
THAT OFTEN COMES TRUE.
IF WE'D EXILED HER, THEN ...
THIS WOULD NEVER HAVE HAP-PENED.
FOR SIX YEARS ...
HER HATE FOR HIM KEPT GROWING, I GUESS.
AULOX?
KILLED?!

BAROSSO !!
WHAT
ARE YOU UP TO NOW?

BAROSSO, NO.
IT'S BLASPHEMOUS!!

S-STOP.
NO.
NOT HERE!
IT'S JUST AN ICON.
IF GOD REALLY EXISTS, IT MAKES NO DIFFERENCE WHERE WE DO IT.
IN THE CHAPEL,
BEFORE THE ALTAR...
IT'S ALL THE SAME.

WITH SINUOUS FORCE
BAROSSO REPEATED IMMORAL, CARNAL ACTS.
I FOUND MYSELF CAUGHT BY THE POWERFUL STIMULUS AND SWEET TEMPTATION OF SIN.
I WAS AFRAID OF BEING CAUGHT AND EXILED FROM THE MONASTERY. YET AT THE SAME TIME...

...LET MY INNOCENT SISTER BECOME INVOLVED.

BUT THE WORST THING I DID WAS...

HE WAS SO QUICK.
THE MOMENT I REALIZED WE WERE CAUGHT, BAROSSO HAD HER.
TO KEEP HER MOUTH SHUT,
HE RAPED HER AND DRAGGED HER DOWN INTO OUR GODLESS WORLD.
I...
...DIDN'T EVEN TRY TO STOP HIM...
I JUST STOOD THERE, FROZEN..

THAT WAS MY BLOOD, THE GIRL HE PUSHED DOWN AND VIOLATED.
AND THAT WAS ME, WATCHING IT HAPPEN.

MICHELLE ?!

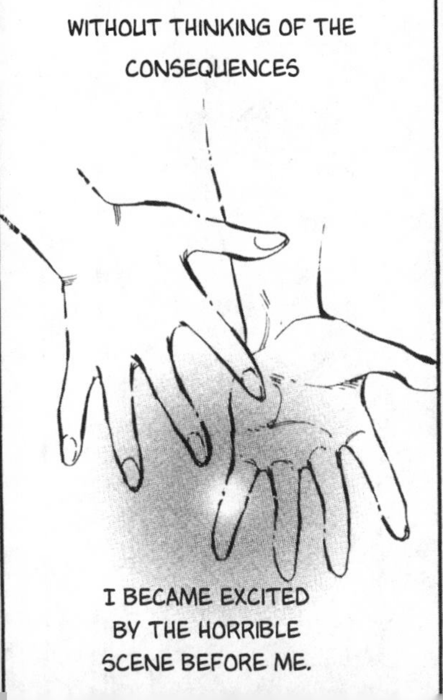
WITHOUT THINKING OF THE CONSEQUENCES
I BECAME EXCITED BY THE HORRIBLE SCENE BEFORE ME.

EVEN RICHELLE'S SCREAM
WAS LIKE A SWEET SONG TO ME.

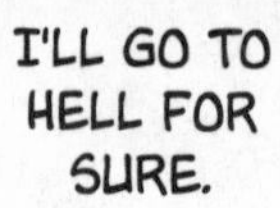
I'LL GO TO HELL FOR SURE.

I WILL NEVER...
MAKE LOVE TO A MAN OTHER THAN BAROSSO.
KLAAANG

HI.
MICHELLE.

NNNNG

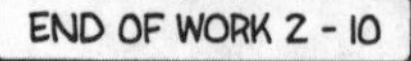
END OF WORK 2 - 10

WORK 2
The Village of Stone 11

KLANK
KLINK
FWIP
UGG
FWIP
FWIP

KYEEE
KYEEE
KYEEE
WHISH
SWISH
KYEEE
KYEEE
SO LOUD.
EYE-BATS.
THEY KNOW THEY'LL HAVE MEAT SOON.

NGG
SKWEEZ
CLANK!
THIS IS THE FETUS RIPPED FROM TEOLA AULOX'S BELLY!!
AND THE SWORD USED TO CUT HER!!

THEY LOOK FOR NON-MUTATING HUMANS ALL OVER THE WORLD.
THIS IS WHAT THEY REALLY ARE!!
THEY COLLECT LIVING CELLS WITH NORMAL GENES FROM THE OLD WORLD!
THAT'S THEIR TRUE MISSION!
A LIFE BORN OF HEALTHY PARENTS.
A BABY THAT HASN'T KNOWN THE OUTSIDE WORLD!
THAT'S THEIR HIGHEST PRIZE!!
KILLERS WHO WILL RAVAGE A MOTHER TO GET AT HER CHILD!!
AND BUJOLD WISTABLE WHO HIRED THEM FOR REVENGE AGAINST MR. AULOX!!
SEND THESE BASTARDS TO HELL!!
YAAHHHHHH!

WHAT ?!
BAROSSO IS INCITING THE VILLAGE PEOPLE ?
THOSE MAIDS WOULDN'T DO...
SUCH A HORRIBLE THING!
MR. AULOX CAME IN HERE
'CAUSE BAROSSO'S DRUG WASN'T WORKING.
HE WAS DYING ...
EVEN THOUGH HE WAS TAKING N.O., RIGHT?
THEN...

IF MR. AULOX
SAID THE PILLS WERE PHONY ...
BAROSSO COULDN'T SELL THEM HERE ANYMORE, COULD HE?

MANUELLA!
YOU SHOULDN'T SAY SUCH A THING!
NO MATTER HOW MUCH YOU HATE BAROSSO!

THE ONE I HATE IS...

YOU...

MANU -
I HATE YOU BECAUSE YOU LISTEN TO HIM!!
I DON'T GET IT.
HOW CAN YOU LOVE A MAN LIKE THAT?
THEY'LL BE LYNCHED.
I DON'T KNOW THESE GUARD MAIDS.
I NEVER MET THEM.
BUT THEY'LL BE KILLED WITH MOTHER AND RICHELLE !!
SLASHING THE MOTHER'S BELLY?
PULLING A BABY OUT?!

HOW
COULD
THEY ...

FLUMP
GLUNK
MY ...
MICHELLE!!
I'M OKAY.
BLUSH
PEGENTO...
DO YOU ...
...LIKE MANUELLA?
WHAT?
UM
WHAT?

YOU WANNA TAKE OVER A PUB?
HUH, MANUELLA?
THIS DOPEY BOY...
WAS ALWAYS WITH ME. HE MAY NOT HAVE NOTICED.
HE-
HEY!
WHAT ARE YOU TALKING ABOUT?!
WITH PEGENTO,
YOU TWO CAN MANAGE.
YOU HAVE PHOTOGRAPHY SKILLS.
MICHELLE !!
I BURNED THE MAID OUTFIT.

KEE KEEKEEKEE
GYAK
GYAK
GYAK
GYAK
GYAK
GYAK

DON'T FRET, ICHELLE.
I WON'T LET YOU DIE.
!!
SQUISH
YOU WITH YOUR HABIT. SOME NUN.
JUST LIKE MICHELLE, YOU ARE DRAWN TO SIN.

GRRMBL
I'LL GIVE YOU AND MICHELLE A GOOD TIME.
AFTER THIS IS DONE.
GYAK GYAK
KEKEKE
GYAK GYAK GYAK
KEKEKE
PUT ME DOWN !!
DAMN IT!

SARAI!!

KLIK
WE'LL BLOW YOUR HEAD OFF!
LET KELZ DOWN!
FWIP

WHA-
THOSE EYES!
THEY'RE THE EYES OF ONE WHO HAS SEEN LIFE AND DEATH TIME AND AGAIN AND SURVIVED COUNTLESS BATTLES.

THE MOB WAS QUIETED BY A PRESENCE UNNATURAL FOR A TEENAGE GIRL.
ALWAYS READY TO DIE FOR HER MASTER, A GUARD MAID IS NOT AFRAID OF A HUGE CROWD.
SUDDENLY CALMED DOWN.
WHAT HAPPENED? THAT ANGRY CROWD

SHHHHHHHHHH
THE CALM BEFORE ...
SARAI ....
A SILENCE THAT CAN EXPLODE WITH ONE COUGH.
BAROSSO SHOUTED
SOMETHING.

SARAI
!
GET
HER!!
KILLER
MAID!!
GOT
YOU!
END OF WORK 2 - 11

WORK 2
The Village
of Stone 12

HOLD IT!
WAIT!
GYAAAAAAAAA
STOP!
STOP!
WHA-
WHAT?!
NYA AAH

HUH?!
THOK
KRAK
WHAK

FWIP
WAAAAAA
CRACK!

AAAAAAAAAAAAAAAA
THWUMP!
THE BUILDINGS A WRECK.
SORRY
RESCUED THE CLIENTS!!
MADE IT!
MADAMS !!

FLICKER !!
HOLD IT RIGHT THERE.
SURRENDER, SARAI.
I ADMIRE YOUR COURAGE IN COMING BACK HERE.

HEY!
DON'T YOU CARE ABOUT YOUR PARTNER?!
KILLING PEOPLE AND STEALING A FETUS.
THAT'S JUST THE KIND OF THING
YOU PEOPLE FROM OLSO DO!!
YOU REALLY...
TALKED A GOOD GAME, DIDN'T YOU?
MR. AULOX CAME TO MOTHER FOR HELP.
DUE TO BAROSSO'S "N.O."...
MR. AULOX WAS BECOMING A PEGMATITE!
EVEN IF WE WERE ENE-MIES...
HOW COULD WE KILL HIM...
WHEN HE CAME TO US FOR HELP?!

SIDE EFFECT?
WHAT ABOUT A PEGMATITE?
MR. AULOX ASKED MOTHER FOR HELP?
HUH?
OR ANYONE WHO TAKES BAROSSO'S DRUG!
IT COULD HAPPEN TO YOU ...
IF YOU'RE NOT CAREFUL, YOU'LL TURN INTO A STONE ZOMBIE
JUST LIKE THE REST!

DON'T LISTEN TO HER!!
THEY'RE ALL LYING!
MY DRUG HAS NO SIDE EFFECT!
DO YOU BELIEVE...
THESE WITCHES AND KILLER MAIDS?!
WELL?!
DO YOU?!
WE BELIEVE.

MANUELLA !!
THIS IS THE SWORD THAT KILLED YOUR PARENTS!
HUH ?
AND LET YOU SEE HER ESCAPE FROM THE WINDOW.
HE MADE A CERTAIN WOMAN DRESS LIKE A MAID
TO LAY BLAME ON THE MAIDS ...

....
THAT'S THE SWORD ....
BAROSSO !!

Shove
Slash!

FLICKERRR
!!!

COME OUT, BAROSSO!
IT'S USELESS TO HIDE NOW!!
DAMN!
RMBL
RMBL
RMBL
YOU CAN'T HIDE FROM US!
COME OUT!!

DON'T DIE, FLICKER !!
I'LL OPERATE !
ARE YOU ... CRY-ING?
SARAI ?
SHUT UP
IT'S DEFINITELY HOPELESS.
IF YOU OPERATE ON ME,
YOU ARE SECOND CLASS IN EVERY WAY...
GIVE ME A BREAK.
I SHOULD'VE LEFT YOU GAGGED.
IDIOT !!
QUIET!
DYING IN THE LINE OF DUTY IS A HIGH HONOR.
IF ONLY IT WERE THE OTHER WAY AROUND ...
HA. IT WASN'T SO COOL, THOUGH.
OH, WELL...

WHA …
WHAT ARE THEY?
ARRGH !
THESE ARE THE THINGS THAT SCARED
YOUR FATHER.

THUMP!
AAAAHHH
GAAH!
GASP!
ZH
ZH
ZH
WAAAAAAAAAAAA

WHERE THE HELL IS HE HIDING?!
DAMN IT!
AAAAAHHH!
K-CHOOOM!
END OF WORK 2 - 12

WORK 2
The Village of Stone 13

Huff
Huff
Huff
Huff
Huff
BLAP
AH!
BUMP
EH?

KRK
KRAK
BLLIP
KRRAAK

YAA!
ZHZH
ZHZHZH
YAAAAH !!

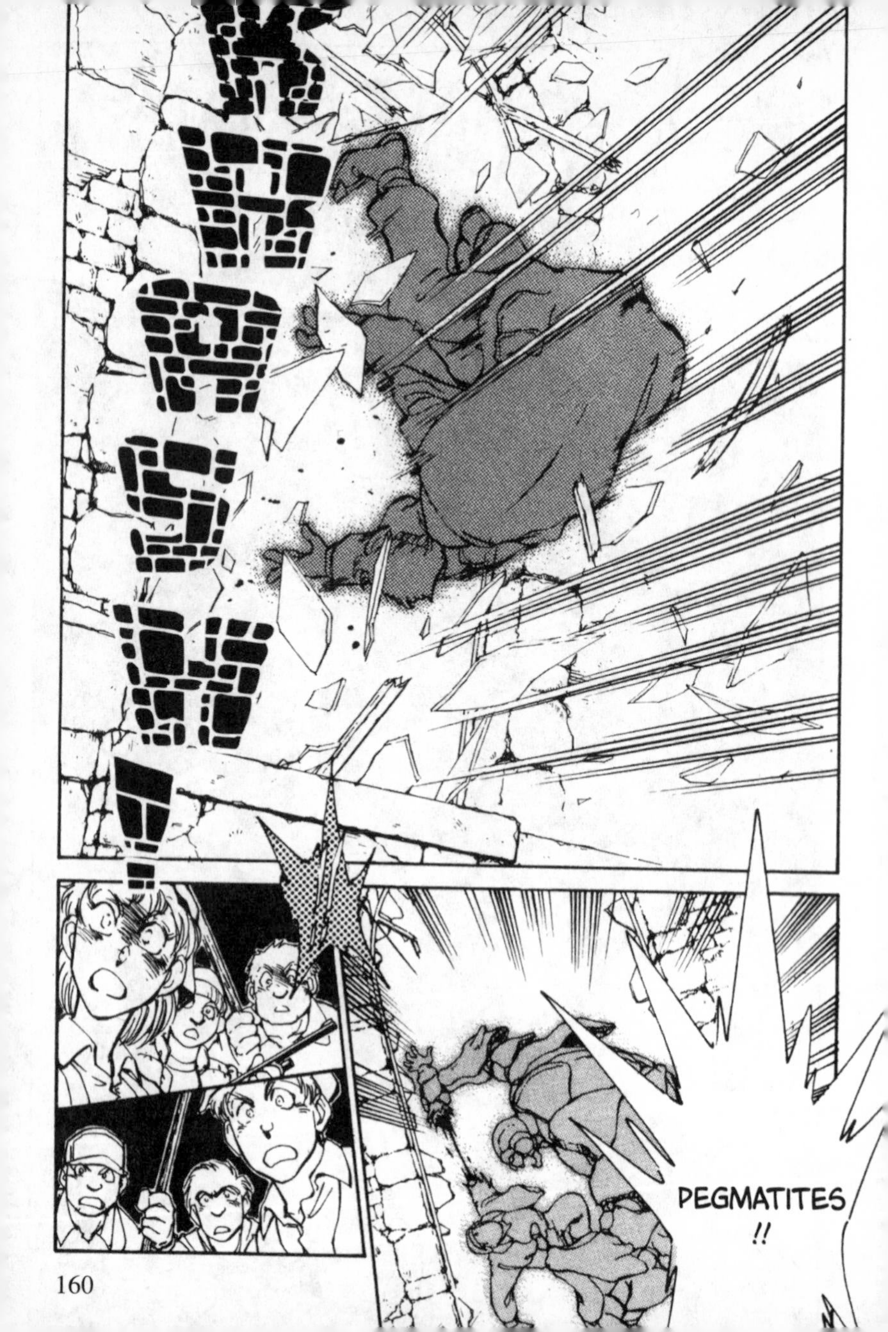
PEGMATITES
!!

WHUDD
KRAK
KRAK
KRAK
SKREEECH!!
BLAM
BLAM
KTHANG!
KTHANG
KTHANG
AIEEE!

THUM
THUM
THUMP
MOTHER!!
THOOM
HURRY, SARAI!
OK...
ONE MORE STITCH...
BANDAGE, PEGENTO!
SKREEK
HERE!
SKREEK
SKREEK
THEY'RE HEEEERE!!
SKREEK

BRAKKA
GLAK
GLAK
GLAK
GWAAAAAAAA
MOTHER!
PEGENTO!

HEH HEH
WAHAHAHAHA

HOW DO YOU FEEL ...
... KNOWING THAT YOUR BLOOD WOKE THEM UP?
ARE YOU STILL ALIVE, GYU?
IT WAS YOUR BLOOD!

SKWEEK
SKWEEK
SKWEEK
IT WASN'T UNTIL MUCH LATER THAT WE REALIZED IT MIGHT BE BECAUSE OF THE DRUG.
WHEN THEY FIRST ARRIVED
THEY WERE RELIGIOUS AND KEPT THEIR HUMAN MINDS FOR A WHILE.
THEY WERE TRAPPED IN NIGHTMARE BODIES THAT COULD NOT DIE.
SO THEY CAME HERE FOR HELP.
IT WAS HORRIFYING.
IN THEIR LAST HOURS, PEOPLE WENT TO THE VALLEY OF SANCTUARY AND RETURNED AS MONSTERS.
THIS SHOULD NEVER HAVE HAPPENED.

IF THE VILLAGE PEOPLE HAD LEARNED THE TRUTH, IT WOULD'VE BEEN CHAOS.
SO MOTHER CHOSE TO HIDE THEM.
THOSE WHO CAME BACK TO ASK FOR HELP, SHE PUT TO SLEEP WITH HER POWER AND SEALED THEIR ANGER AND DESPAIR.
AND ALL OF A SUDDEN ...
...WE HAD LOTS OF THEM.

RUN!
BAM
BAM
BABAM

GYAK
GYAK
BWAT
GYAK
HUH?
KIKI KIKEKEKE
KIKEKEKEKE
EEEEE
EEEE
MY EYES!
GYAAA
JUST ...
JUST LIKE BEFORE!
LIKE THAT NIGHT
THE EYEBATS ATTACKED US!!

BAM!!

THEY AREN'T LOOKING TO BE SAVED ANY-MORE.
ONCE THEY FIND HER, THEY WILL KILL HER.

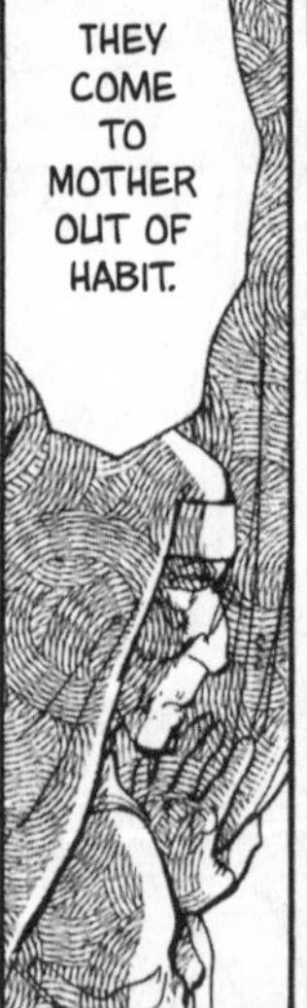
THEY COME TO MOTHER OUT OF HABIT.

SINCE THEN, PEOPLE LOST FAITH IN RELIGION.
THEY ARE JUST MON-STERS NOW.
THE PEG-MATITES HAVE NO HUMAN MIND LEFT.

GOD BE WITH YOU.
UH
YOU WANNA FIGHT 'EM WITH THAT?
SKWEEK

THIS WILL BE...
...THE END OF FIOLITO.
RMBL
RMBL

CLONK!
FWAP
THEY MUST BE FROM OUTSIDE.
CAME OUT TO JOIN THE PARTY WHILE THE SUN'S STILL UP...
EVEN WITH YOUR POWER ...
YOU'RE NO MATCH FOR SO MANY PEGMATITES.
IT'S HOPELESS, SARAI.

FWAP
FWAP
FWAP
LOOK!
THEY'RE EVERY-WHERE!
WE ...
WE'RE SURROUNDED !!

AAAAAAAAAA
CHOM!
YEEB
THUD THOOM
EVERYONE!
GET BACK!

BACK TO THE BUILDING ?!
B- BUT
THAT'S WHERE THEY CAME FROM !
YOU WANNA GET RIPPED APART HERE ?!
'COS THEY...
GRRAR
... WOULD BE HAPPY TO DO THAT!
RRROARR
WHA... RICHELLE ?!
WELL, YOU CAN USE THE HELP, CAN'T YOU?
END OF WORK 2 - 13

WORK 2
The Village of Stone 14
RICHELLE
!

PLEASE GO BACK !!
IT'S ALL RIGHT AS LONG AS MOTHER'S SAFE!!
BUT WE'RE HIRED TO PROTECT YOU!!
I'M NOT GONNA LIVE LONG ANYWAY.
WE'LL COVER YOU, PEOPLE !!
RICH-ELLE
I'M NOT AS HELPLESS AS YOU THINK!
KSHUNG
I KNOW THE PEG-MATITES' WEAK POINTS.
AND BESIDES

QUICK !!
INSIDE !!
FWAP
FWAP
FWAP
BWAT
AIIEE !!
ARRHH !
WHKOOM
GYAAAA
GYAK
GYAAAAAA

THIS WAY!!
HURRY !!
RUN!
GYAAAA
GYAAAAA
KSHACH
TOO MANY OF THEM!
DUMB FLICKER!
YOU ARE REALLY USELESS!!
AT A TIME LIKE THIS!

CLOOMMM!!
CRASH!!
KRAK
KRAK
KRAK
THEY CAN'T FOLLOW US UPSTAIRS!
HURRY, HURRY!!

KRAK
KRAK
KRAK
THWAM!
ULP
THUM!
WAAH!
THUD!
ULP!
WAAH
!
DUMM!
WAAAA
WAAA

KSHANG
KSHANG
WHY WON'T IT OPEN?!
KSHANG KSHANG
SKEEK SKEEK
DAMN IT!
BAM
BAM

WHY CAN THAT BASTARD RUN AWAY
AND I CAN'T?!
KLLANG
GULP
SKREEK
SKREEK
Ahuh Ahuh

WHOO
DOM!
CRMBL
CRMBL
CRMBL
WAH
WAH
WAAAAAHHH!
CRK
CRAK
SKEEEEEEK
BOOM
KOFF!

FRANTZ
SORRY TO SCARE YOU.
COME WITH ME.
IT'S ALL RIGHT NOW.
NOTHING TO WORRY ABOUT.

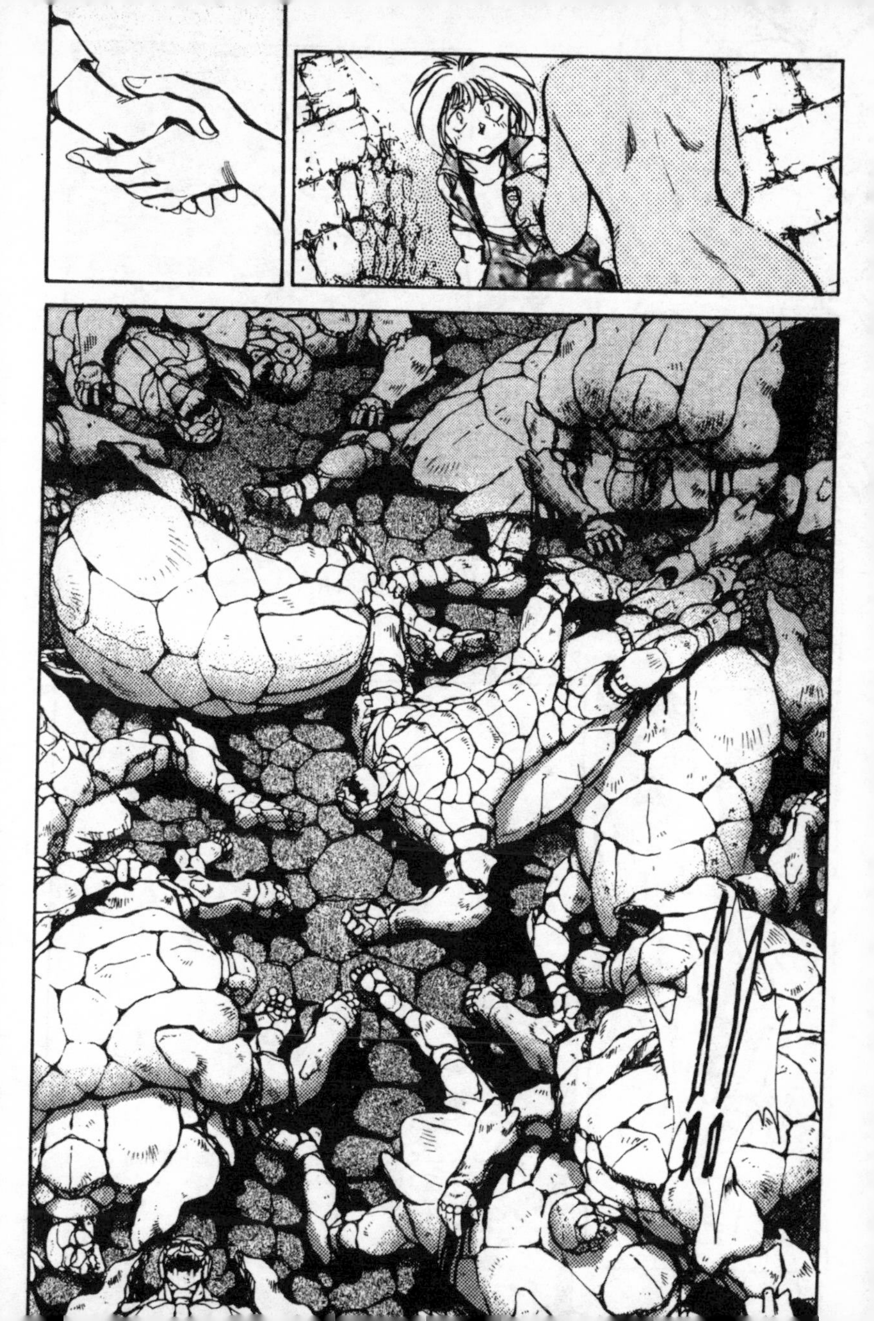

Y..
YOU ...
YOU DID THAT ?!
!?
FLICKER ?!
FF
KKLIP
KKLOP
KKLOP

MICHELLE !
WHY?! WHY?!
BAM!
KLANG
KLALANGG
KLALANGG

BAM
GOODBYE, BAROSSO. I LOVED YOU MORE THAN ANYBODY IN THE WORLD. I REALLY DID.
I WAS CAPTIVATED BY YOUR BODY AND SOUL.
I COULDN'T RESIST YOU AT ALL, BUT I FINALLY FELT GUILT FOR MY WEAKNESS...
IT'S... NOT POSSIBLE !!
AND IN THE END, I TURNED AGAINST YOU. FORGIVE ME...
CRACK
SKID

THWAK
FWAP
FWAP
WHDD
CLOSE YOUR EYES, RICHELLE !!
SARAI ?!
SA

HUH?

MOTHER
!!

I AM THE ONE TO BLAME ...
FOR CREATING THESE MONSTERS.
?!
BAROSSO'S DRUG ...
WAS ORIGINALLY MADE FROM MY LIVING CELLS.
I'M SORRY, RICHELLE ...
AND I THANK YOU
FOR SERVING ME UNTIL THE END.

MOTHER!!
MOTHER!!
LET ME GO!
NOOOO!
MOTHER DIED IN AN INSTANT.
BUT THEN
AN UNEXPECTED THING HAPPENED.

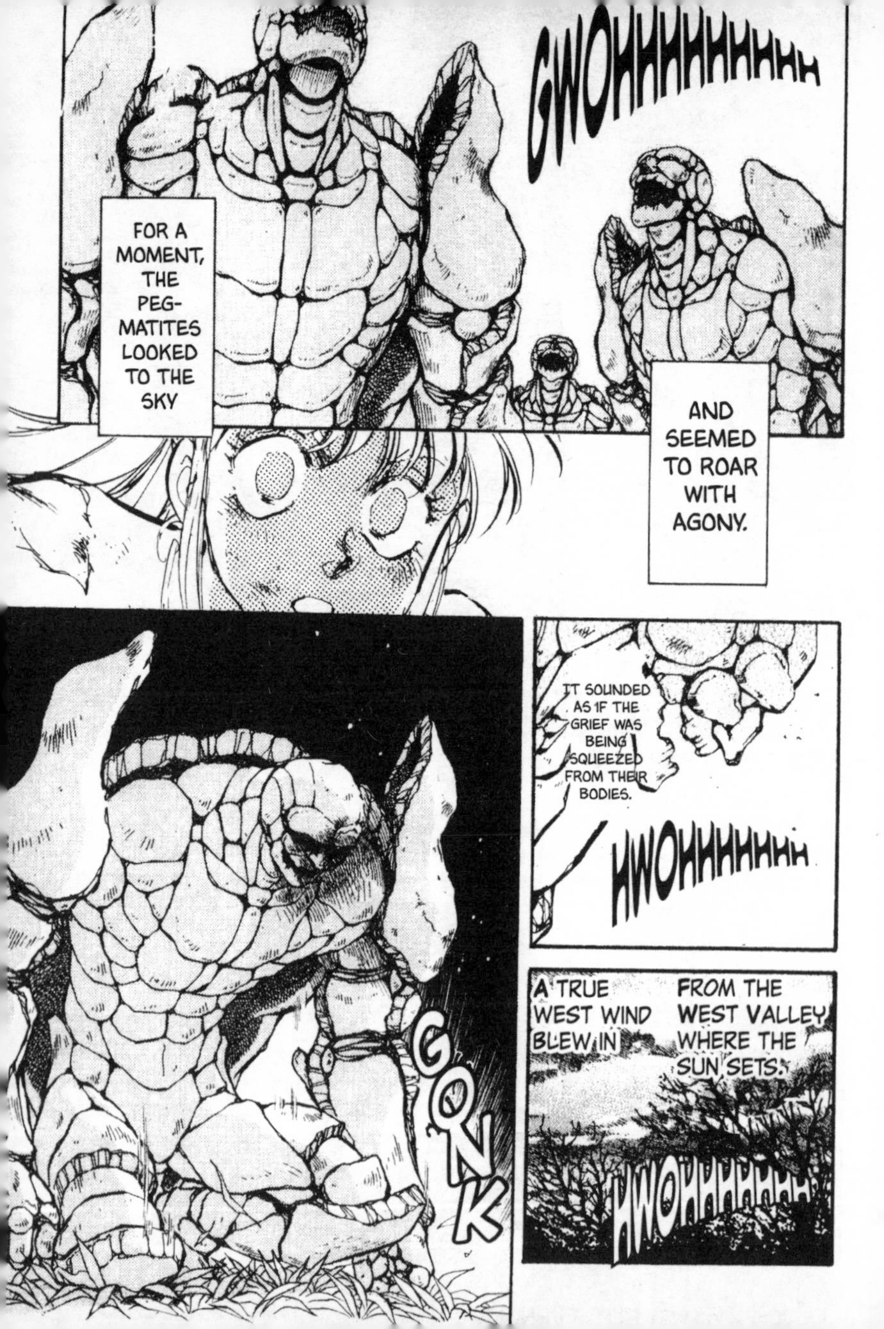
GWOHHHHHHHH
FOR A MOMENT, THE PEG-MATITES LOOKED TO THE SKY
AND SEEMED TO ROAR WITH AGONY.
IT SOUNDED AS IF THE GRIEF WAS BEING SQUEEZED FROM THEIR BODIES.
HWOHHHHHHH
GONK
A TRUE WEST WIND BLEW IN
FROM THE WEST VALLEY WHERE THE SUN SETS.
HWOHHHHHHH

IN THE GOLDEN LIGHT SHINING OFF THE GARDEN OF RUINS
THE PEGMATITES COLLAPSED ATOP ONE ANOTHER.
IT WAS AS IF THEIR SOULS WERE TAKEN TO THE LAND OF ETERNAL SANCTUARY, LED BY THE WEST WIND.
MOTHERRRR!!
MOTHER!

THIS IS MY NIGHT-MARE...
WHEN I DIE,
ALL BE OVER.
N.O. WAS MADE OF HER OWN DNA. PEGMATITES WERE MOTHER'S ULTIMATE DEMON.

PERHAPS WHAT AULOX BELIEVED WAS CLOSE TO THE TRUTH.
REALLY ?!
WAS SHE HERE ...
ALL THIS TIME ?!
SHE ALMOST DIED.
DUE TO YOU KNOW WHO!
HOW CAN SHE MOVE?!
THIS IS IT!!
THIS IS THE HAND !!
?
?
GYU ?

HWOHHHHH

KMOKKKKKKKKKK

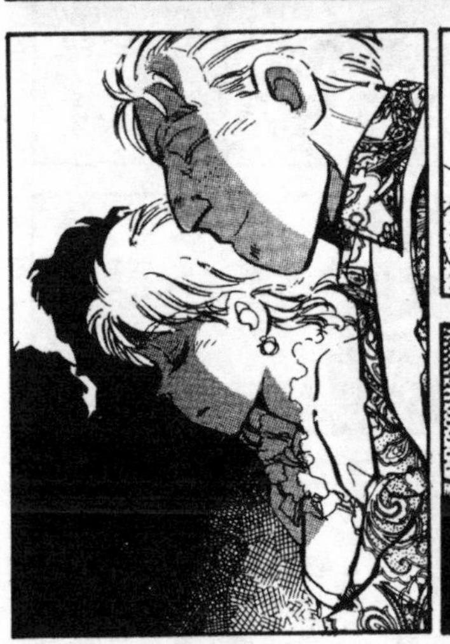

HUFF
HUFF

MICHELLE!!
OPEN YOUR EYES!! MICHELLE!!

LET ME HEAR YOUR VOICE!!
MICHELLE!
GRASP
OPEN YOUR EYES!

PLEASE, OPEN YOUR MOUTH!!
TAKE THE PILLS!!
TAKE THESE!
OPEN YOUR MOUTH!
YOU'RE STILL WARM!
SAY SOMETHING!
YOU CAN HEAR ME, CAN'T YOU?!

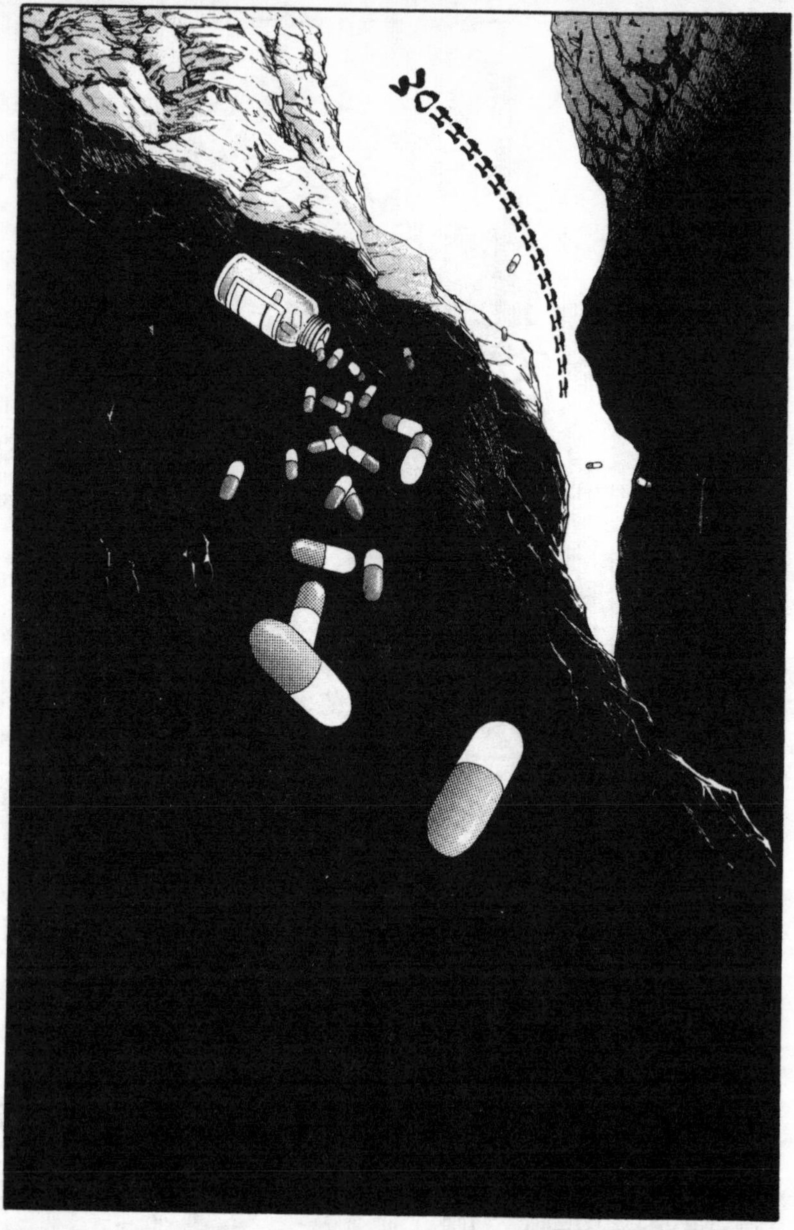

END OF WORK 2 - 14

END OF SARAI VOL. 2

TO BE CONTINUED IN

SARAI VOL. 3

JESUS by Yoshikazu Yasuhiko

Jesus. Teacher, healer, savior. The story of one of the most revered figures in human history is revisited in this full-length graphic novel, featuring breathtaking full-color art by Yoshikazu Yasuhiko.

*Volume 1-2 are available in ebook format.
*200-207 pages each

JOAN by Yoshikazu Yasuhiko

Emil is a young woman who may be the second coming of Joan of Arc. Following visions of Joan, Emil undergoes her own mission to unite a feudal France under the divine rule of the King.

*Volume 1-3 are available in ebook format.
*183-223 pages each

KAZAN by Gaku Miyao

Kazan is a boy warrior searching for his childhood companion on a desert planet. Magic and swordplay accompany Kazan and his friends on the road to the legendary land of Goldene.

*Volume 1-3 are available in ebook and hardcopy formats.
*187-201 pages each

MAICO 2010 by Toshimitsu Shimizu

Maico's a charming young woman who also happens to be an android--and the sexy new DJ of Japan Radio! She ends up entangled in a human love triangle, plenty of scandal and intrigue surrounding the station, and a mysterious military organization that wants her dead!

*Volume 1-3 are available in ebook and hardcopy formats.
*184-209 pages each

TOMIE by Junji Ito

Tomie is the girl you wish you could forget. She is the one you shouldn't have touched, shouldn't have smiled at, shouldn't have made angry. She is quite lovely and you just might love her to death.

*Volume 1-2 are available in ebook and hardcopy formats.
*220-248 pages each

WEED by Yoshihiro Takahashi

Weed is a courageous little dog who believes he's the son of the legendary Boss Dog, Ginga. After his mother dies, Weed begins an adventurous journey to find his father in the Okubo Mountains.

*Volume 1-3 are available in ebook and hardcopy formats.
*238-240 pages each

comics
ONE

comics
ONE